Vacation to Graceland

Phillip Cornell

First published by Dog Ear Publishing
4011 Vincennes Rd
Indianapolis, IN 46268
www.dogearpublishing.net

ISBN: 978-1-4575-3738-7

This book is printed on acid-free paper.

Printed in the United States of America

CHAPTER 1

The idea of a family trip started, when my mom devised a plan to take my granny on a weekend trip. This was difficult because my granny was on a weekly dialysis schedule, so my mom had to come up with a way to keep her schedule and transport her from one city to the next without any problems. My grandma had been on dialysis for the past 2 ½ years, and with her increasing age and decreasing health she needed more attention from care givers and family members.

The living arrangement in my mom's house was setup like this. My mom, my sister Brandi, and my granny all lived there constantly. My other sister Crissy and her children did not live there, but they would visit often. I myself would visit quite often also. My job was 2 miles from my mom's house so it was nothing for me to visit on my lunch break or when I got off work. My granny anticipated me coming over many times, so she would cook a meal for me, and place my name on the plate. It was not the perfect living arrangement, but it definitely had a strong family feel tied into it.

My granny kept close tabs on what my mom and sister was always doing, because that is just who she was. She still liked to get out the house ever once in a while. Her favorite pastime was people watching. If there was one thing that she enjoyed, it was talking about other people. This is a trait that has been handed down from generation to generation, and I myself am guilty of doing it also. Discussing people in a humorous light that downgrades their physical appearance or personality is second nature to me now. I can easily do it without any effort or stress. The thoughts just come to my head, and I let the mild form of slander flow. I have never been embarrassed of this, and like me, my granny was neither.

Seeing that my granny did not like to be left out on a traveling experience, my mom knew that if she was to try to go anywhere out of town, she had to bring her. If my mom left without my granny, then my grandma would shun her for not including her on the trip. One time my mom did sneak out of town. She left with her best friend to plan the funeral of her friend's brother. My mom knew it was going to be a problem with my granny, so she did not tell her until she was already on the road. When my granny found out my mom left her, she threw a fit and started crying. My sister Brandi tried to explain to her that the trip was for business and not pleasure, but my granny did not care. She just knew that my mom was out on an adventure without her.

Knowing all of this information, my mom knew the next time she left town that my granny was coming no matter what. She called the dialysis center and my grandma was scheduled for dialysis the day before they left for the trip, and the day after they returned home from the trip. My mom was not sure how everything was going to work out, but solidifying my granny's dialysis schedule was the most important thing. Once that was done, then the trip as a whole was a green light.

One day while I was stopping by my mom's house after I got off work, my mom asked me if I wanted to go with her to a family reunion in Memphis Tennessee. I had never been to Memphis, so I agreed to it just for a new experience. My mom told me that it would be $25 to attend the reunion and that my transportation and housing would be taken care of. In my mind, I saw it as me having a free trip. I had absolutely no worries.

My mother and I had the conversation about the family reunion in late May. I asked my mom what weekend I needed to take off of my job. She told me the weekend after the 4th of July, so I requested the days off and had it set in my mind that I would be visiting Memphis at some point in time in July. When the month of July was very close I decided to look at my job schedule to see if I had the right days off. Somehow I managed to take off the wrong weekend. I noticed this mistake exactly 2 weeks before the departure date. I immediately told my boss about my mistake and she and I scrambled to get my shifts covered for the correct dates. Between the both of us we were able to get the right shifts covered, and I did not have to lose the shift I had originally taken off a month previously. I only had to take off one shift to make the trip, but that one shift was enough to throw me for a spin.

After fixing my requested time off I decided to take the trip more seriously. I asked my mom how we were going to get to Memphis and who all was going. She told me we would be driving in her Nissan Murano that was a 5 passenger SUV. She then told me the passengers of the vehicle would include her, my granny, my sister Crissy, and her 2 children. One of Crissy's children was 8 years old and the other was 6 years old. I immediately counted the number of people attending the trip on my fingers.

After I was done counting I noticed 6 people including myself would be riding in my mom's SUV. I was confused seeing that her SUV comfortably holds 5 people, and we were fitting 6 people into it. I asked my mom about the travel arrangements, and she got a whole attitude with me. She asked me if I wanted to drive my car, and that I was welcome to spend my money on gas if I wanted to. This made me mad, because I did not sign up for this. We lived in North County in St. Louis Missouri. The trip to Memphis was going to take us 4 ½ to 5 hours to reach our destination. I asked my mom how she thought that piling 6 people into her SUV was a good idea. My mom told me that she had fit 6 people into her SUV before, and that my nephew Chaz does not take up that much space. I asked her where she went with the 6 people in her car. She told me that she went to Outback Steakhouse. The Outback Steakhouse was at most 15 minutes from her house. She looked at me in my face and compared a 15 minute car ride to a 5 hour road trip. Now at this point I was no longer mad I was angry. I could not see how this comparison was valid, but somehow it made perfect sense to her. I told my mom I would look into getting a Mega Bus ticket, and I would get back with her on if I would be riding with them to Memphis. After that statement I decided to leave it alone, because no matter how much I argued with my mom there was no way of showing her the error of her logic.

I just bided my time until it was the day of the actual trip. I did not successfully find a Mega Bus ticket because I did not look. I had all intensions of looking for a Mega Bus ticket, it just did not happen. Now I was stuck in the crowded car full of people. I could not complain because it was my fault. I still gave my mom a hard time about the full car of people all the way up until the trip. Every time she heard me complain she would rebuttal by saying that I could drive if I wanted the leg room that the driver seat had. She knew I would decline, but I would entertain her request every once in a while. I knew there was no escaping the long and gruesome tip to Memphis that I was about to take.

On the actual day of departure my mom told me to meet at her house at 12:00 noon. I was told Crissy had to work that day, and we were going to pick her up from her job downtown. After we got her, we would leave immediately from her job and head towards Memphis. This sounded perfect to me. I got a good night sleep, and packed my bag that morning. I was accustomed to packing, so the process of double checking my bag was effortless. The most important thing about packing is making sure you have a complete toiletry kit and one more pair of underwear and socks than you actually need for the trip. I always carry at least one pair of long pants and one pair of shorts. I then make sure I have a jacket or a hooded sweatshirt. You can look at the weather forecast all you want, but there is no guarantee the weather will be like the forecast predicted upon arrival.

I dressed in some basketball shorts and a t-shirt. I also put on one of my most comfortable pair of shoes. I dressed like this because I am a firm believer that while traveling you should travel as comfortable as possible. I made sure my phone was fully charged, and that I had a pair of good headphones with me. There was no way I was going to be caught in an overcrowded vehicle without my headphones. That was not an option for me. I grabbed my bag and shoe box, then left my apartment and headed over to my mom's house.

I had not gone on a family trip in years. It was mostly because I had gotten older and grown into adulthood. I just wanted to travel with my friends more than with my family. Another reason was because my dad died of colon cancer 7 years previously, so the trips I use to enjoy as a child could not be relived without him being there physically. My mom, dad, Brandi, myself and whoever else wanted to tag along would go on a family trip once a year. We went to all types of places even Canada. Once I became a teenager I started going on 2 week long hiking trips with my dad through the Boy Scouts of

America. This took the place of the traditional family trips, but I was still with my dad. When my dad was diagnosed with cancer, all the focus went to him beating the disease. Once he died, we mourned as a family and found a way to piece our lives back together. One of the ways of doing this was learning to enjoy ourselves without him being around.

My mom, Brandi, and I lived in the house for a year adjusting to our new life then I left for college. While I was at college my mom told me she was getting rid of my room and my grandma was moving in. My granny was a widow also, so the loneliness both of them had could be subsided by each other and the company of their children. For my granny it was my mom, and for my mom it was Brandi. Before my granny had kidney failure and had to go on dialysis, my mom, Brandi, and granny went on a trip to the Bahamas without me. They did not tell me until 2 days before they left. My mom wanted to make sure the dogs were fed, and that I let them out to use the bathroom when they needed to go. This sucked because I wanted to go, but I was more concerned about making money at my job then spending time with my family in the islands. It was a decision I made, but I got over it. I assumed there would be more trips, but my granny got sick and the whole idea of going on another family trip just vanished.

Now that my mom found a way to work around my granny's sickness, I was headed to my mom's house trying to embark on a trip to Memphis. When I turned down my mom's street I noticed something that would set the tone for the entire trip. My mom lives at the bottom of a long street that ends in a cul-de-sac. Her house and about 5 other homes form the cul-de-sac. As I drove down the street, I see my granny joy riding on her scooter around the cul-de-sac. I had to dodge her on the scooter in order to pull into the driveway. The garage door was already up, so I hoped out of my car and put my luggage in the back of my mom's SUV. I then walked in the house to see what was going on.

I was confused. My grandma was in the cul-de-sac riding her motorized scooter for fun, and my mom was trying to make sure everyone's luggage was properly packed into the back of her SUV. My mom started sewing a couple of months prior as a hobby. She was really not all that good at being a seamstress, but she was rapidly improving at her craft. She made an outfit for my 8 year old niece Bria to wear, but it did not fit her right. Bria was modeling the outfit for my mom and Brandi when I walked in the house. They were trying to figure out how they could fix the outfit, so she could wear it on the trip. After deliberation between the both of them, they decided to go to K-Mart and buy Bria an outfit to replace the outfit my mom had sewn together.

Once this decision was made my mom looked at me and said, "You and I are going to go to the store!" She said we are going to get what we need, then come back home immediately. I agreed because I did not have a choice. My mom and I then walked to my car in the driveway. When we got to my car my granny pulled up on her scooter. The garage door was still up, and my granny told my mom that she wanted to take the scooter with her on the trip. My mom said, "Huh?" My granny repeated that she wanted to take the scooter with her on the trip. My mom then looked at me, so I took that as a clue to unpack the SUV and repack it with the scooter in the back of it. I broke down my granny's scooter and took everything out the back of the SUV. Good thing Crissy had already dropped her and the kid's luggage off at my mom's house the night before, so I knew how much stuff actually had to go in the back of the vehicle. I packed everything back into the SUV with the scooter at the bottom, and it surprisingly fit.

When I was done my mom told me lets go before we run out of time. We still had to pick up Crissy from work, and my mom did not want to be late. When my Granny heard my mom say let's go, she asked where we going. My mom said to the store. Then my granny asked if she could come. I immediately said no. Every time my granny goes somewhere with us it makes a 20 minute trip into an hour long trip. I knew this was going to happen, so I tried to avoid it. My mom told me that I could not tell my grandma no. She then told my granny to come on, and we all loaded into my car. I shook my head because I knew what was about to happen.

During the drive to K-Mart we passed the liquor store. My granny pointed to it and said, "Stop! I got to get me some tickets." My granny was addicted to scratch off tickets. She would win sometimes, but she mainly did it for recreation. She claimed every 2 months that she was going quit, but then she would get the itch and had to play her scratch off tickets. My mom told her no and that we would drop her off at the grocery store to get her some tickets. Her plan was for us to drop her off at the Shop N Save, and we would get what we needed from K-Mart. Then we would pick my granny up from Shop N Save. This plan made sense because the Shop N Save was in the same plaza as the K-Mart. This enabled us to kill two birds with one stone. I told my mom it was a scratch off machine in K-Mart, but she insisted it was not. I did not argue with her because I was not 100 percent sure myself. I dropped my Granny off at the Shop N Save then my mom and I went to the K-Mart.

When we entered the K-Mart my mom went to the clothing department to find some clothes for Bria. I went to the outdoor section to find some bug spray. Apparently when my mom went to Memphis 10 years ago, the place where we were having the barbecue had a really bad tick problem. Brandi told me I needed to find a bug spray with a higher than regular percentage of deet in it. I searched the outdoor section of K-Mart for about 10 minutes before I found the bug spray. I called Brandi to confirm I was getting the correct bug spray then I set out to find my mom in the clothing department. When I found my mom she was already in the checkout line. She did not text or call to me to tell me she was done. She just hopped in line and waited on me to find her.

I joined my mom in line, and put the bug spray with the items she was purchasing. When we made it to the cashier, the cashier informed my mom that she had $50 in reward points. My mom started talking with me how Crissy could use the money on school supplies for my niece and nephew. I listened to her to be courteous, but I did not really care. I was ready to pick my granny up and get the road trip started. My mom made her purchases then we started to leave the store. While we were nearing the door I saw a scratch off machine for the Missouri lottery. I told my mom I knew K-Mart had a scratch off machine, and my mom looked at the machine and laughed. She then stated my Granny would not have liked the tickets in it anyway. I looked at the tickets inside the machine and I reluctantly agreed with her.

My mom and I got back to my car and drove up to the Shop N Save. My granny was sitting on the bench outside the store waiting on us to pick her up. She had already scratched off all the tickets she purchased. She threw away the losers and put the winners in her handbag. After I helped my grandma get into the SUV we went back to the house. We were gone for about 50 minutes. It was not quite an hour, but it was pretty close. I did not complain. I just rolled with the blows and kept on moving.

Upon arriving at the house we double checked we had everything we needed for the trip. After everything was checked my mom told everyone to get in the SUV. Chaz was eating some ice cream out of a cup when my mom said this. Because he was eating some ice cream, Bria wanted to eat some ice cream. Chaz was nearly done eating so Brandi told Bria no. She told her she had to leave with us, and there was no time for her to eat any ice cream. My mom did not allow Bria or Chaz to eat in her SUV, so if Bria did not already have the ice cream then she was not going to get it. This conversation between Brandi and Bria happened in the garage next to my mom's SUV. Shortly after Brandi told Bria no, my granny walked out the house with a plate of ice cream eating it. My mom and Brandi looked at her with the same look. It was the look that she knew better than to be eating ice cream in the SUV also. My mom saw my granny then said, "Dang! We got to wait for her to finish her ice cream." She told Bria she could go get some ice cream, and we waited for everyone to finish their helpings. When everyone finished their ice cream we set out on the road to pick up Crissy from work.

Brandi decided not to go with us on the trip. She told me she was going to have the house to herself, and have plenty of alone time. Brandi was happy she did not have to watch Chaz, Bria, or my granny. I asked her before we left if she could wash my car. She actually agreed without any extra incentive, and I thanked her in advance. I personally hate when people make plans for me on my off days, so I know Brandi being my sister is the same way. Brandi did not work or go to school. She was strictly a caregiver for my grandmother. Crissy would use Brandi to babysit and help with Chaz and Bria when it was convenient for both of them. Between all this babysitting and being a caregiver, this trip provided a nice vacation from responsibilities for her. All Brandi had to worry about was having the house clean when my mom returned home, and now making sure my car was washed.

CHAPTER 2

During the car ride my mom decided to stop at the bank before we picked up Crissy. I sat in the back of the car with Chaz and Bria. They had their hopper devices, so this entertained them for a total of 5 minutes. After losing interest in her hopper, Bria immediately asked to see my phone. I told her no! We had a conversation a week prior about how I was not going to let her use my phone. Bria remembered this conversation, and asked my mom to see her phone. My mom gave it to her with no second thought. Bria took the phone and went straight to YouTube. Chaz and her both loved YouTube. They literally could look at YouTube for hours upon hours.

Bria was the bigger one out of the 2 children, so when there is an argument between them Bria uses her size advantage to get her way. Bria searched around YouTube for 2 minutes until she found something she liked. Chaz could see her being entertained, so he put his hopper down to peek over her shoulder. Bria turned her shoulder and shielded the phone away from Chaz so that he could not see it. Chaz was fine at first then he started to complain about Bria not sharing.

My mom told the children to stop arguing then she pulled up to the bank and went in. After she left the car, Chaz tried again to look on the phone Bria had in her hand. Bria shielded it from him again then Chaz started crying. My granny saw Chaz crying and she told Bria to give him the phone. Bria told my granny that she asked for the phone first, and Chaz did not want to see the phone until she had it. My granny said she did not care, and she made Bria give up the phone. Bria reluctantly did it then started crying herself. My mom came back to the car and took her phone from Chaz. She said that if they did not know how to share then no one can see the phone. Both of the children cried for about 45 seconds then they got over it.

The rest of the car ride was a continuous argument between Chaz and Bria. When we got to Crissy's job we pulled out front the building. We waited a couple of minutes then Crissy came out. She had a large carrying bag that she placed in the back of the SUV. She then went to the driver's side of the car. My mom got out the car, and crammed into the backseat of the vehicle with me, Chaz, and Bria. The car was now at full capacity, and we were ready to begin the road trip.

When my mom got into the backseat, she sat between Chaz and Bria. This cut all the bickering and fighting in half. I was actually mad! Why did I not think about sitting between them? I guess as a parent you learn some things from experience. Crissy, also being prepared, pulled out 3 pairs of headphones from her bag. She used one for herself then gave the other 2 pairs to each of the children. Bria took hold of my mom's phone, and Chaz took Crissy's hand held tablet that she had with her. The children were quiet, and everyone either had headphones plugged in or were entertained by leisurely conversation inside the SUV. Everything was now at peace, and we began our drive to Memphis.

About 18 minutes into the car ride, I noticed we were headed out Interstate 40 West. From taking a quick look at the directions on how to get to Memphis from St. Louis, we were supposed to be driving on Interstate 55 South. Driving on 40 West did not make sense seeing that we left from downtown St. Louis. It was not like we were taking a detour either. There were plenty of opportunities to get on 55 South from a magnitude of locations. I decided to ask where we were going when I came to the realization that we were traveling further and further West. My sudden outburst interrupted the conversation my mom, Crissy, and granny were having. All 3 of them looked at me simultaneously after I blurted out my question. Crissy then said she had to pay a bill before we left out of town.

At this point I was thinking that that we would never leave the City. We were doomed to pretend like we were leaving for Memphis, but never achieve our goal. I put my headphones in my ears, switched to an extended playlist on my phone, and just enjoyed the ride. When we stopped at the destination that Crissy drove us to, I got out the car to stretch my legs. I had been riding in the car for 30 minutes and my legs were stiff. I did not want to imagine how they would feel after the 5 hour car ride. Crissy finished paying her bill, and everyone crammed back into the SUV. Then we officially started our ride to Memphis.

My mom had the idea for me to sit behind the driver's seat instead of the passenger's seat. My granny had the passenger seat because she was the oldest one in the car, and she had the right to whatever seat she wanted. Seeing that Crissy was short, she had to move the seat up really close to the wheel in order to drive. This left me a significant amount of leg room which I was grateful I had. Once the leg room problem was solved, I still did not have much arm space. I propped my right arm up around the top of the backseat. It was not the most comfortable position, but it gave me room to expand my body. Bria sat next to me, and she did not complain that much. She just wanted leg room so she could twist and turn to reach for snacks out of the back of the SUV. Bria sat next to my mom, and Chaz sat next to her. This was the spatial arrangement for the first part of the trip.

I had not eaten the whole day, and I was absolutely starving. Brandi gave me a piece of some short ribs she had before I left my mom's house, but that was not nearly enough to nourish a person of my physique. I asked my mom if we were going to be stop anytime soon. My mom said the plan was to stop at Lamberts Café: Home of the Thrown Rolls. I got immediately excited! I had not been to this restaurant in years, and I was eager to go back! About 50 minutes from Lamberts Café, my mom received a phone call from our cousin Yvette asking her where she was. My mom told her we got a late start to the trip, and we were still on the road. Yvette told us to hurry because they were having a fish fry that afternoon, and if we made it to Memphis in enough time we could attend the event.

In theory we were 3 ½ hours from Memphis. I could not wait that long! Besides the piece of Brandi's short rib,

I had not eaten in 16 hours. When my mom got off the phone, I told her to stop me in the city of Cape Girardo. I made up in my mind I was getting some fast food in the next 30 minutes! My granny heard everything that was happening, and she said we were going to Lamberts Café and that was final. Once granny spoke, it was set in stone.

We drove another 40 minutes then pulled up to Lamberts Café. It was everything I remembered it as being. It was a large building oozing with tradition. There were people lined outside the establishment underneath a sign that said "Welcome to LAMBERTS CAFÉ (The Home of the Thrown Rolls)" Crissy stopped the SUV close to the entrance. Then she and Chaz got out, so she could make reservations for the family. My mom then climbed into the driver's seat, and drove the SUV in search of a parking spot. My mom initially looked for a handicap parking spot to accommodate my granny, but there were none available. My mom decided to just let my granny out the car close to the entrance with Bria then she drove around the side of the building and found a parking spot.

When my mom let Bria out the car with my granny, she told both of them to stay put. My granny of course did not listen, and started walking to the inside of the building. This included her having to dodge a few people, step up onto a porch, and walk through some double doors. Bria did not help her one bit. When I was able to get out the car and find the both of them, my granny was about to run into some little girl that was playing on the edge of the porch. I immediately grabbed my granny's arm and guided her through the entrance into the restaurant. I then showed her where the waiting area was, and I sat with her while we waited on my mom.

Crissy found my granny and me in the waiting area, and told us it was going to be a 25 minute wait to be seated. We all shrugged our shoulders and settled in. During the wait, Bria and Chaz initially occupied themselves with all of the hanging pictures and antique pieces that surrounded the waiting area. The pictures were of people from the early 1900's, and the antique pieces were replicas of cooking utensils used during that time period also. After Bria and Chaz studied the pictures and antique utensils, they discovered the arcade.

I went with the children to see what the arcade had to offer. My mom gave them both a dollar to play the games. Bria spent her dollar on a boxing game that lasted 15 seconds. She then asked me for another dollar. I gave it to her and she put it right back in that boxing game. She came back to me 15 seconds later looking for a dollar to give to the money eating game. I looked her in the eyes and told her no! I went to see what Chaz was doing, and he was playing a driving game that was lasting quite a long time. He then played a basketball game that seemed like it lasted forever. Chaz had the right idea. He used his little money to have the most complete and long lasting experience he could possibly have. Bria on the other hand wanted to play on the most elaborate looking game, whether she knew how to play the game or not. She had intensions to do this if she got the money from me, my mom, or Crissy.

When Chaz finished playing the basketball game and was out of money, we left the arcade and went and sat by my granny in the waiting area. Bria stayed in the arcade for a bit longer then came out to the waiting room. She asked everyone for some money again, and all I could hear was a consistent no being said to her as she went down the line of people. She eventually gave up and sat down, while Crissy lectured her on how she needs to be more conservative with her money. Shortly after that our parties name was called, and we were seated.

The hostess led us to a table that had a booth styled setting. When I say this, I mean there was a table in the middle of us, and the seats were connected on either side like a booth. You could sit on either side of the table, but there were no seats at ends. My family slid into the booth style seats with my granny and me getting the end of the table that opened into the isle on the right. Chaz and Bria sat in the middle seats, and my mom and Crissy sat at the other end of the table that opened into the isle on the left. This arrangement worked mostly because Chaz and Bria were closed in on both sides by adults.

Immediately upon being seated a waitress came to our table and asked us what we would like to drink. I got the lemonade, Chaz and Bria got sprite soda, Crissy got water, and my mom and granny got coffee. When the drinks came out they were in enormous mugs. My mom seeing the size of the mugs started griping at my granny about how she needs to watch her fluid intake. With my granny having kidney failure and being on dialysis, if she took in too much fluid between treatments she would become sick and struggle to breathe. My granny was well aware of this, but she did not care. She would drink whatever she wanted. If she got sick, she would have someone take her to the emergency room. My mom having dealt with my granny before knew how she was. She tried to monitor her fluid through griping and questioning her constantly. Using this method of control my mom was determined for my granny not to get sick while we were out of town.

The griping from my mom continued sporadically throughout the first part of dinner. The fact that the drinks where in super sized mugs really did not help the situation. Crissy monitored her kids and how much they drank. She did that mainly because she did not want them to drink too much, and we have to stop multiple times on the way to Memphis. Eventually my granny had enough of the gripping! She told my mom she was not going to drink all the coffee in the mug, and she could manage her fluid intake herself. Upon hearing this, my mom looked at my granny then everyone else at the table with a look of disinterest. She then said that sick people should stay at home. My mom made her statement and left it at that.

We did not order our meals when the waitress brought us our drinks, so after we got our drinks we sat at the table conversing for a bit before the waitress came back to take our orders. I ordered a fried pork chop which was a Midwest delicacy. Everyone else ordered a variety of foods that ranged from shrimp pasta to a hamburger. I specifically remember what my granny ordered. She got a chicken pot pie! My granny was obsessed with pot pies. She literally would eat chicken, turkey, and beef pot pies 1 to 3 times a day. Knowing this, when she ordered a chicken pot pie I found it humorous. You would think a person would get tired of the same meal day in and day out, but my granny was not the average person.

After we ordered, my family talked amongst ourselves until the rolls came out. The rolls were hot and ready to be thrown. Bria and Chaz lit up with excitement and anticipation. I could not see myself, but I am sure I had the same glare in my eye as both of them. They were not really concerned with actually eating the rolls. They just wanted them to be thrown at our table. Both of the children raised their hand and the waiter launched 2 rolls over our way. Chaz caught 1 roll and I caught the other one. We divided the rolls between our table and they were amazing! They were hot, soft, and the roll itself melted in my mouth. I almost inhaled my roll because I was hungry and it was that good!

After we called for more rolls and another waiter offered us some free appetizers, I began to fill up. The rolls were pretty filing themselves, but the free side dishes did a number on me. I was nearly full and I had not even received my meal yet. I decided to stop eating until the main course arrived.

Bria being on the chunky side was greedy when it came to food. She was exactly like Brandi and I when we were little. We did not eat until we were full, we would eat until we got sick. Bria was the same way. If her eyes saw it, she would try to eat it and save it all for herself. She kept calling for rolls and catching them. The more rolls she got, the more pressure it was on me to help her eat all of them. Since I was physically the largest person at the table, I had the responsibility of cleanup. I could not take the pressure of consuming all this bread! After the 5th role I told Bria to stop calling for rolls. She said, "OK" and ate her free appetizers and side dishes, along with the pieces of rolls she already had in front of her.

Shortly after the end of the roll fiasco the main dishes came out. I liked most of my food except the greens. I did not like them because they were strictly turnip greens. The greens my granny made were a mixture of turnip, collard, and mustard greens. My mom loves turnip greens, so I gave my portion to her. My meal was tasty but I could not finish it. I ate as much as I could. I made sure I saved the candy yams because they were the best dish on my plate. I called for a few more rolls, and packed me a "to go" plate.

My family sat for almost 15 minutes at the table after we finished our food and received our "to go" plates. I am positive we did this because we needed some time to digest our food before we headed back on the road. My granny paid for the entire meal, and everyone else at the table was responsible for the tip. I put $5 towards the tip because that was all the cash I had. My mom gave me the "you are so cheap look" and pulled $20 out of her purse. I really did not care how she felt. I gave all the cash money I had. That was the way my finances were set up at that point and time.

We then left the restaurant to continue our trip to Memphis. On the way out Crissy took both the kids to the restroom one last time before we left. My mom darted out in front of everyone, and pulled the SUV out front the establishment. We all piled into her vehicle, and set out on the road full and eager to get to Memphis Tennessee.

During the second part of the day long road trip, we needed to stop and get gas in Arkansas. This meant my granny would have another opportunity to buy and play some scratch off tickets. My granny had not scratched in a while, and she needed her fix once again. The exact moment we pulled in the gas station and parked the SUV. My granny made movements to get out of the SUV, and make her way into the gas station.

Other people got out of the SUV also. Crissy and Bria went inside the gas station with my granny, Chaz used the public restroom, and I got out the SUV and walked around. My mom filled up the gas tank. After she finished pumping the gas, she printed out her receipt and stuffed it in her pocket. My mom told me previously she wanted to keep track of the trips expenses for her personal records. Once everyone accomplished what they needed at the gas station, we got a good stretch in and headed back on the road.

Bria sat next to me in the backseat again. She kept trying to listen to what I was playing on my phone. Seeing that Crissy was sitting right next to her this time, she knew she could not get away with listening to something she was not supposed to be listening to. I remember that occasionally throughout the rest of the trip, Crissy would look down at the phone Bria had in her hand to see what she was looking at on YouTube. Crissy told her specifically Chris Brown, Justin Bieber, and definitely Miley Cyrus was off limits. She said that some of Justin Bieber's songs would be OK, but any songs by any of the musical artist she mentioned would have to be approved by her. I thought everything Crissy told Bria was funny. This was probably because I was grown, and my mom hated my music selection with a passion.

I managed to sneak a nap in on the back half of the drive to Memphis. The sun started going down, so my mom called our cousin Yvette to tell her that we were not going to attend the fish fry. She told her we were still on the road, and that we would see her and the rest of the family tomorrow.

After the phone call we reached Memphis County fairly quickly. My mom had not plugged the hotel location into her GPS, so she started fooling around with it while she was driving. She does not use her GPS that often, so as a second measure she told me to put the hotel address into my phone. I did what she instructed, but the directions were a bit confusing to follow on my Google maps app. Getting frustrated my mom decided to exit the highway, and try to plug the directions into her GPS while the car was parked.

This was a good idea, except the sun had already set. We were parked somewhere in Memphis, at night, and lost. My mom pulled on a gas station parking lot and began to input information into her GPS. She was not the most computer savvy person, so it took her a while to figure out all she needed to do to get her GPS to work. It was slightly complicated because you could not simply type in the address. You had to pick a region the destination was in. Then select the state. Then you could plug the address into the GPS. We had never used the GPS outside of Missouri, so we did not know all this had to be done.

It took a while to figure out the GPS, and the whole time I was looking around at my surroundings. It was not that hard to tell that we were in the hood! When I say this, I mean that we were in a high crime area that looked sketchy and unsafe. In cities like Memphis these areas are mostly associated with the black community. Knowing this I saw a multitude of black people outside, at night, just walking. I did not know where they were walking too, and honestly I did not care. The gas station parking lot was nearly empty. There was one car on the lot and our SUV was parked in the corner of the lot facing the street. This concerned me, because in St. Louis if a gas station in the hood was vacant at night that meant something happened to defer people from coming. A murder or robbery was usually the reason.

At this point my spidey senses were going out of control! I was zeroing in on everything that moved relatively close to the SUV. I told my mom we had to leave the parking lot immediately! I told her I did not think we were in a good neighborhood, and I was not sure if we were safe. My mom chuckled and asked, "How did you know?" I responded by saying, "LOOK AROUND!" My mom surveyed the surroundings then quickly got the GPS in order and drove off the lot.

Somehow my mom set her GPS to take the street, and avoid major highways. She did not know how she put this feature on, and she did not know how to cut it off. I still had the hotel address plugged into my phone, so if we got lost using my mom's GPS then we definitely had a backup plan. We followed the GPS and it showed us a lot of the city of Memphis. It was mainly urban communities, but the closer we got to the hotel the scenery gradually started to shift to suburban communities.

CHAPTER

3

Our hotel was located about 35 minutes from downtown Memphis. It was in a place called Germantown. When we pulled out front the entrance to the hotel, my mom put the SUV in park and exited the vehicle. Her and Crissy got out the car and went inside to check in. My mom told me to get into the driver seat, and park the car in a parking spot if someone came up behind me. I listened to everything I was told, and patiently waited for my mom and Crissy to come out of the hotel and give me further instructions.

After waiting for 15 minutes, I was wondering why it was taking my mom and Crissy awhile to come outside with the key cards. By this time another car pulled in behind me. I decided to park the car in a nearby parking spot and wait it out there. I plugged my headphones into my ears, and waited for my mom to call me to tell me what the word was. I waited for about 2 songs then cut the car off.

My granny, who was still in the SUV, became restless. She asked me where my mom was. I told her she was still in the hotel doing something. My granny then told me to drive back around to the entrance of the hotel. Listening to my granny, I put my foot on the brake and pressed the push to start button. Nothing happened. This was because my mom had the key in her purse, which was with her inside the hotel. My granny saw me try to start the car, and when it failed she asked me what the problem was. I told her my mom had the key on her, and she had to come outside for the car to start. For some reason my granny did not believe me. She started fussing and said that us kids were so tied up with our little computers (phones) that we did not know how to do anything or listen. She then tried to push the start button herself and nothing happened. She called my mom herself on her cell phone that was an ancient relic from the year 2004. When my mom answered, my granny told her to come outside.

Knowing that my mom had no idea where the SUV was parked, I called my mom on my phone. I told her I cut the car off, and needed her key. My mom was already outside, so I got out the SUV and started waving my arms to show her where we were parked. My mom spotted me and walked up to the SUV. The first thing she asked me was why I moved the SUV. I told her that she was taking all day, on top of a car pulled up behind me. This led me to make the decision to move the vehicle to a parking spot. My mom said, "OK" then I started the SUV and pulled it back around to the entrance to the hotel.

Crissy came out of the hotel and we began to unload the SUV. When I got into the hotel I saw what took my mom and Crissy so long to check in. Instead of us having 1 room for everyone, we had 2 separate rooms. My mom, granny, and I had one room, and Crissy and her 2 children had the other room.

After everyone's luggage had been loaded into the rooms, I asked my mom how the 2 room situation happened. She told me that when she booked the hotel on Expedia.com, the description of the room said it had 2 full beds and a couch that let out into a bed. With that arrangement everyone except 1 person would have a bed to sleep on. Her plan was for me to have the let out bed to myself, Crissy to share a bed with my granny, and Chaz and Bria to have the other bed. My mom had volunteered herself to sleep in a chair. This plan actually would have worked, but I highly doubt I would have let my mom sleep in a chair and she was financing most the trip. When we arrived at the hotel, the room that was offered had one full bed and a couch that let out into a bed. My mom being disappointed and mad told the concierge that the hotel provided false advertisement. She mentally prepared herself to cancel her reservation and go to a completely different hotel. Crissy not wanting to look for another hotel asked the concierge how much for another room. The concierge told her the price of the room for the weekend, and she took it.

My mom not liking Crissy's decision agreed to the new terms and kept her mouth closed about the manor. The concierge seeing that somewhere it was a mistake made on his hotels behalf gave Crissy a free bottle of wine. This was a meaningless gesture, but none the less Crissy accepted the free alcohol and paid for the extra room.

When we settled into the hotel room, my mom made a phone call to Brandi. She told Brandi about everything that happened at the hotel, and made a comment that Crissy is spending money like she is not broke. She went into how Crissy spent money on an extra hotel room, and how she brought some unneeded items out of the gas station in Arkansas when we stopped. She ended her conversation by saying that she was not going to question Crissy on her trip finances, but she was going to keep a close eye on her the rest of the trip.

When my mom got off the phone she made sure my granny was properly ready for bed. Sharing a room with my granny was awkward. There was one point where she changed into her pajamas, and just did it over by her bed. There was really no privacy in the room, so out the corner of my eye I could see her in nothing but undergarments. It did not take me that long to get over the awkwardness. It was something I expected, but the first minute or so was very intense.

Once my granny climbed into bed, she took control of the only T.V. in the room. My mom settled down, took some of her medicine then asked me if I wanted to go to the bar with her. When we got to the bar, my mom ordered a beer and asked me what I wanted to drink. I looked at the liquor selection and was not impressed. I saw some Jack Daniels, so I ordered a Jack and Coke. The bartender did not have Coke so she poured my Jack in some Pepsi. I did not complain because my mom was paying for my drink. She asked me, "When did you start drinking Jack Daniels?" I think my mom would forget I was 25 so she was always astonished when she saw me drink hard alcohol. I just chuckled, and told my mom it was the only alcohol I could stand out of the selection in front of me.

My mom and I talked with the bartender for about 10 minutes then we both finished our drinks. We walked back to the hotel room and I text this girl I knew who lived in Memphis. I told her that we could hangout on Saturday, because I was tired from Fridays travel. She texted back saying, "OK" then I went back to listening to music on my phone.

My mom shared the bed with my granny, and she left me the bed that pulled out from the couch. She put her pajamas on, and told me to come with her to mess with Crissy and the kids. I went with her to Crissy's room which was located directly next to ours. When we knocked on the door Bria answered. She asked us what we wanted, and my mom told her to let us in. Bria moved out the way and we walked in the room.

Crissy had the whole bed to herself along with the T.V. angled in the direction of her bed. Chaz and Bria were sharing the couch that pulled out into a bed, and they were watching a movie on Crissy's laptop. Crissy had her room nice and cozy. My room was not like this. My granny had me cut the air conditioner off immediately once she walked in the hotel room. I told my mom I cut the air conditioner off, and she said she would handle that problem after my granny went to sleep.

We talked with Crissy for a bit then went back to our room. My granny was half awake watching some show about prisoners in a medium security prison. The show profiled 4 to 5 different prisoners each episode. It focused on how each person had adjusted or was adjusting to life in the penitentiary. This show was OK, but after 1 episode I was done with it. I swear it was a marathon going on, and my granny wanted to watch every episode. Every person on the show had some messed up reason why they were in prison. A couple of guys wanted to be rappers, another wanted to be a barber, and someone else was furthering his education. Like I said, the show was OK. I could only take so much.

I finally got tired enough to go to sleep. I put my phone on the charger and curled up in the pull out bed. The bed I slept on was amazingly horrible! I could feel the springs of the bed in my back. I tossed and turned constantly! I would have rather slept on the floor. At least there I would know what I was getting myself into. I found some way to sleep, but I knew I would have a stiff back the next day.

When I woke up my back was feeling horrible. I stretched to alleviate the stiffness I had accumulated throughout the night. I put on the clothes that I would be wearing for that day. I did not know what the day's plans were, but I was sure that we would be attending a Barbecue. I pulled my shoebox out from my personal pile of luggage. I asked my mom if I should wear my Jordans to the Barbecue. She told me my relatives lived in the country and there was going to be a lot of dirt. I took this as her indirectly telling me that if I wore my sneakers to the barbecue that they would get dirty.

Me wanting to keep my shoes as fresh as possible knew that kicking my Jordans through the dirt would anger and disappoint me at the end of the day. Those particular shoes I had paid a lot of money for, and they were not easy to come by. I had to wake up extremely early the week before the release day. The shoe store I tried to get my shoes from was releasing raffle tickets. In order for me to purchase the desired shoe, from that store, I needed a raffle ticket. My roommate worked at the shoe store. He told me to get to the store inside the mall at 8:00 am. He said the manager would release the tickets at 10:00 am, so if I got in line that early I would be guaranteed a ticket. This was a good idea, but the store he worked at was in a mall that was a 45 minute drive from my apartment. This meant I would have to leave at 7:00 am to get to the mall, and navigate my way through it to get to the shoe store by 8:00 am.

Somehow I got up in enough time to make the long drive to the mall. I also made it to the entrance of the shoe store by 8:00 am. When I got to the store I noticed there was no line outside the gate. I assumed I was the first one there. My roommate was not working that morning so I tried to call to him to ask him what was going on. I also noticed that the shoe store directly across the hall had a line of 60 people outside. I was still confused so I looked through the gate into my roommate's shoe store to see if I could see someone inside. I saw a guy through the gate, and he came to greet me by the entrance. He did not raise the gate, but he was nice enough to inform on what happened. He told me he had a line outside his store around 6:00 am and he wanted to get rid of it, so he raffled off the tickets around 7:15 am.

I was greatly disappointed! I knew some people in the line at the shoe store across the hall. I crossed the hall to talk to them, to find out if it was any point in getting in the line they were already in. One person told me not to waste my time because that particular shoe store had only 20 pairs of the desired shoe, and there was clearly more than 60 people waiting in line. Another person then suggested that I go up the escalator to another shoe store, because the line there was not nearly as long. He also said that they have a random raffle, instead of a first come first serve method of dispensing their tickets. Weighing my options I was desperate to get these shoes, so I decided to press my luck with the store up the escalator.

I went to the next level and got in line. I had some leisurely conversation with the people I was in line with.

I text my roommate to tell him about everything that happened thus far. He did not answer my initial phone call, so I assumed he was still sleep. He surprisingly text me back within 15 minutes, and told me the guy I spoke with outside his store was his manager. He then said he was surprised he gave the tickets away so soon, and he would see what he can do to get me the shoes. I did not know what he meant, but I just patiently waited in line. I had sacrificed so much gas and sleep not to be successful. My roommate text me back 30 minutes later saying his friend, who was a manager at a shoe store somewhere else, would be able to sale me a pair she had at her store. I just had to wait 3 days after the release date. I agreed with the terms, and I graciously exited from the raffle line. I had spent 3 hours of my morning trying to get those shoes. When I was able to obtain them, I coveted them like they were a child.

Me knowing how much I like these particular pair of Jordans, I decided not to wear them to the barbecue. I wore the shoes I traveled in the day before. This was a good decision; I just had to make sure my ensemble coordinated because I was wearing clothes I did not plan on wearing that day.

When I finally got dressed, I left the hotel room and went to the pool area. Bria and Chaz had woken up early to go swimming before we left for the day. They asked me if I wanted to swim with them. I declined because I had already gotten ready. If I hoped in the pool I would have to retake a shower, and get redressed all over again. They understood why I said no. Also their swimming session was nearly over. They had to get out the pool and start getting ready themselves.

My granny got a late start on the day. She took her shower before me, but I got dressed way faster than she did. This was probably because she was over 80 years old. Also she had to iron her clothes perfectly. Naturally she started off her day complaining. She did not like the bathroom. My mom cut the air conditioner back on, so she said the room was cold. In general she just decided that the hotel was, in her words, sad.

The setup of the bathroom was weird. The standup shower and the toilet was enclosed in the bathroom. The twin sinks and mirrors were located outside the enclosed bathroom adjacent from the master bed. This meant that you had to use the toilet then open the door and wash your hands. Same thing was the case for the shower. You would take a shower, dry off, then open the door and use the sink and mirrors. All of this was coupled with the space inside the bathroom being very tight. It was not very elderly friendly. My granny had a somewhat difficult time using the shower. The shower head was tightly fit into the wall, so adjusting it up and down, left and right, was not easy for her. The entire setup of the bathroom caused my granny to complain.

Once my granny was ready, we were ready to leave. Bria and Chaz had gotten out of the pool, showered, and gotten dressed. My granny told my mom she was hungry. My mom said we had some time to kill, so it was OK for us to go to a restaurant. We piled into the SUV and drove exactly 1 mile from the hotel. We pulled into a strip mall, and the best restaurant type place we could see was Qdoba. That was just not going to do.

We collectively came up with the idea of asking someone at the hotel were where the surrounding restaurants. This thought process conveniently came 10 minutes after we already left the hotel. My mom did not want to back track so she said lets go to Cracker Barrel. My granny loved Cracker Barrel, and everyone had eaten there before. Weighing the options we decided Cracker Barrel was a safe move to make. I typed Cracker Barrel into my Google Maps, and the restaurant that came up was 27 minutes from our location. My mom told me to check again, and the same Cracker Barrel came up. After about 2 minutes of fooling around with my phone, my mom said, "Oh well! We will make the drive."

We hopped on the highway in route of the restaurant. Along the way my granny told my mom she won some money on some of her scratch off tickets. My mom told her we could stop at a gas station to redeem them. Upon further thought I told my mom to read the back of one of the tickets. My mom read the back of the ticket and it said Arkansas state lottery. This meant we could only redeem the ticket in Arkansas. My mom told my granny and my granny replied by saying, "Isn't Arkansas and Memphis the same thing?" My mom told her no. My granny did not believe her, and she said that she would ask my great aunt Ping if she could redeem the tickets in Memphis.

When we got to the Cracker Barrel everyone was starving. We went inside and were seated fairly quickly. We familiarized ourselves with the menu then began ordering food. My mom told everyone not to order much food, because we still had to attend a barbeque later that day. No one really cared about the barbeque at this point. We were living in the moment.

When our waitress initially came to the table to drop our menus off, she formally introduced herself. She took our drink orders, and came back fairly quickly to take our food orders. When she left the first time my mom looked at me. She did not say anything she just wanted me to read her mind. When the waitress left the second time my mom looked at Crissy and said, "What do you think about our waitress?" I immediately knew were this conversation was going. The waitress was for lack of a better word, dirty! She had on a dirty white shirt, her lips were as black as coal, and she had a couple of teeth missing. She was really nice to us, but she was definitely dirty.

My mom watched the waitress like a hawk every time she came back to the table. She carefully examined her food and everyone at the table food when it came out. Good thing the food was good and it came out swiftly, because I felt like my mom was waiting for something to complain about. Seeing that the experience at the Cracker Barrel went smooth, I was glad we made it in and out with no major complications.

Upon leaving the restaurant the kids used the restroom before we piled back into the SUV. My mom went to the car and my granny went shopping in the antique store in the front of the Cracker Barrel. Every Cracker Barrel had the antique store in the front of it, and my granny was eager to see what this one had to offer. She did not buy anything, but I had to wait for her comb through the store and see everything she wanted to see. While I was waiting with my granny I looked through a picture book of horses to occupy my time. The book was somewhat interesting, but not interesting enough for me to buy.

When my granny was done, I walked her out to the vehicle. Somewhere doing the walk from the restaurant to the SUV I had been bitten by a mosquito. I had this big red splotch on my leg, and I showed it to my mom. My mom told me and everyone else to get the bug spray out the SUV and spray ourselves down. My mom, Crissy, Chaz, and Bria went insane with the spray. They caked it in on like it was body spray or something. Being a rebel I gave myself a light coat, and my granny followed my lead and sprayed herself a light coat also. I do not know why my granny wanted a light coat, but I personally did not want to smell like bug spray!

My mom plugged the destination to the Barbecue into the GPS, and we headed out. Once we hit the highway we saw a sign that said "Welcome to Tennessee". Everyone in the car was confused. We thought we were in a suburb of Memphis. I then looked at my phone and noticed we had just left Mississippi! We had gone into Mississippi and did not even know it. Now looking back at the clues everything mad sense. I saw multiple Mississippi license plates on the Cracker Barrel parking lot, the Cracker Barrel was really far from the hotel, and lastly the waitress had no teeth. I am not saying that all waitresses in Mississippi are dirty and have no teeth, but if someone told you our waitress was from Mississippi you could look at her and see how that was possible.

Everyone laughed at our own stupidity then we passed a sign that said Graceland the next 2 exits. My mom asked us if we wanted to see Elvis before we went to the barbeque. I spoke for everyone by saying yes! We got off the exit, and it took us a while to find the actual Graceland. There were signs promoting Graceland, but they were confusing. We drove the wrong way for about 5 minutes until we stopped seeing Graceland signs. My mom turned the car around and turned down a different street. This street was the correct street. We saw Graceland on the right, and my mom pulled into the parking lot.

Upon pulling into the parking lot, the security guard told us that parking was $10. He also was very courteous and told us that is was a 2 hour wait to get into the mansion. We did not have time to wait 2 hours. On top of that my granny said she was not waiting 2 hours. In her exact words she said, "DAMN ELVIS!" in her old lady voice. I giggled for a bit then my mom turned the car around and said, "We will try again tomorrow before we leave."

When we got back on the highway, my mom's GPS started acting up again. It had us exit the highway and go through suburban communities. This was pointless! We saw some nice houses and a whole golf course. The GPS was obviously taking us on a suburban tour of Memphis. After 10 minutes of driving, I got tired of the GPS and plugged the desired destination into my phone. Following my phone we were able to use main streets to get us to the barbecue.

The barbecue was at my great aunts Ping's house. People were still preparing the food when we arrived, so we greeted everyone and started to settle in. My mom had previously told me that Ping lived in the country. As I looked around her land and her house, things looked quite developed. There was an actual neighborhood around her house, and there was a grade school that looked fairly new across the street. Initially I was told Ping had a lot of open land, and you could not see the next house from her house. Now there were aspects of the country that still existed. Ping had a gravel driveway. Also her original house was made out of brick, but it was condemned. So sitting next to the house, was a double wide trailer. There was plenty of land for these 2 structures, so I made my observations and kept it moving.

We went inside the trailer to see who was in there. This required me to walk up a long aluminum pathway. When we got inside, it was the same size as a ranch style home. It had a living room, 3 bedrooms, kitchen, and 2 bathrooms. It was basically a house. There was an awkward smell though. I just assumed it was the smell of old people. My granny room has an old person smell, and I smelled it quite often. I guess once you become a certain age, you get used to it.

My granny decided to stay inside the trailer with the air conditioner. I went back outside to sit in a lawn chair. The gravel my aunt Ping had all throughout her property created a lot of dust. I was glad I made the decision to not wear my coveted Jordans. While I was outside, I met some more of my relatives. They were all older than me. They knew my grandparents, uncles, and aunts well, but they did not know me. I mean I did not know them. I tried my best to be social, but the barrier of distant relatives was really hard to break.

After about an hour of sitting in the lawn chair, more people started to role in for the barbecue. The food was almost done, and I started to meet more and more people. The first group of people I met was my mom's 2nd and 3rd cousins. She was familiar with them, but I had never met them before in my life. Sitting in my lawn chair, along with some other people, we formed a half circle. The half circle consisted of Crissy, me, 2 ladies, and 2 men. One of the men stood out as a defined personality. His name was Stanley. He was in his late 40's to early 50's and he was a talker! He told me the other man was his brother, and that one of the ladies was his sister. The lady that was not his sister was his cousin. I did not remember everyone's name, because I have never been one good with names.

The lady that Stanley introduced as his sister brought her dog with her. She explained to me that

Stanley met her in Kankakee Illinois, and they drove from Kankakee to Memphis. Her dog made friends with another dog that was already owned by someone on the property. The 2 dogs were no more than 10 or 12 pounds, and they were constantly playing with each other. Stanley's sister would tell them to quit playing and just get it on. The funny thing about this was that both the dogs were male. She knew this, and she said they were having a homosexual relationship. I looked at how fond the animals were of each other, and all I could do was laugh.

The man Stanley introduced as his brother was slightly older than the rest of the bunch. He was sitting with the group, but he was slightly removed from the half circle. He told me his name, but yet again it escapes me. He did have a couple of interesting stories to tell though. When I first walked up to him to shake his hand, he told me he could not see that well. His reason for his poor sight was because 10 years ago he got robbed. During the course of the robbery he was shot in the side of his head. When he was rushed to the hospital, the doctor did not know if he was going to survive or not. Fortunately for him he lived, but his vision was forever tainted. He continued by saying that he was a brick layer, and that he comes from a long line of brick layers. After that statement he told me that he was going to keep laying bricks until his back gave out just like his daddy.

After listening to this man's story and absorbing all the information, Stanley went and got some shrimp he had been cooking on the grill. He apparently brought his own meat to the barbecue. I guess he had gotten hungry, so he managed to cook his personal food before the rest of the food was complete. The shrimp Stanley went to get was sautéed in a spicy sauce and it smelled lovely. Shrimp is my favorite food, and once I smelled it I could not resist. I was not particularly hungry, but the smell of the shrimp lured me in.

Stanley offered me some shrimp, so I took his offer. When I grabbed one of the shrimp, it still had the exoskeleton on it. Stanley had cooked the shrimp without cleaning them or removing the exoskeleton! He told everyone that is how shrimp is prepared in the Caribbean. I peeled the exoskeleton off my shrimp, and used my finger to split the back open. I then pulled the black residue out the back of the shrimp then began to eat my shrimp. I knew this was not how Caribbean people cooked their shrimp. My uncle was born and raised in the Bahamas and he never offered shrimp to me like that! I knew that Stanley wanted shrimp. He was just too lazy to peel and clean them before they were cooked.

I ate 2 shrimp, but did not eat more for fear of getting sick. While eating my shrimp I met another person that was closer to me in age. He was 21 and was wild and rambunctious. He reminded me of my 22 year old nephew who had not come on this trip. This person's name was Tae. He told me he was from Detroit. He was heavy into designer clothes, and dressed as if the name on his clothing was more important than the actual fashion of what was being worn. Tae's outfit was somewhat comical. He was wearing True Religion swimming trunks, but he was not going swimming. If that did not make sense, he strung a Gucci belt through the novelty belt loops in his overpriced swimming trunks. To match his trunks and belt, Tae had on a Hollister shirt and a snap back ball cap. His shoe game was nice though. He had some low top Nike shoes that were smooth in design. My overall critic of his outfit was that he was a designer whore. I never mentioned to Tae, my thoughts on his clothing selection. I just assumed he would grow out of his designer infatuation someday.

I use to dress this way, before I progressed to wearing and supporting designers who clothing made me feel comfortable as a person. I mostly support independent clothing lines because many of them look at clothing as art, and not just a trend. Also I like to get my money worth out of my clothes. I have no problem buying expensive clothes, just as long it is worth the money I am paying for it.

When I initially met Tae, I talked with him about where I was from. Me being from St. Louis and him being from Detroit, we connected on both of us being a kid from the semi big city type of thing. After getting to know him and the other people I was sitting with, I was ready to go on a liquor run. The host of the barbecue had thought to bring everything except liquor. I asked my mom if I could drive her SUV to go to the liquor store, and she surprisingly said yes. She gave me the key to her vehicle. Crissy gave me $20 and told me to get her and the kids something to drink while I was on my run.

When I mentioned the liquor store, Stanley immediately volunteered himself to go with me, because he knew where the liquor store was located. He asked me if his brother could join us, and I was fine with that just as long as there was room in the SUV. I was not going to tell him no. Even though I had just met him that day, we were technically related to each other. Tae tagged along with us, and I had assembled a crew to retrieve liquor.

We got into the SUV 4 people deep, and pulled out of the gravel driveway. 30 seconds into the trip Tae asked if I was familiar with any Detroit rappers. I said, "No!" The only rappers I knew from Detroit was Royce Da 5'9, Emeniem, and Big Sean. Any other person was not on my Hip Hop radar. Tae explained to me that it was way more good rappers in Detroit than the 3 I mentioned. He insisted I listen to the one he had on his phone. Tae took my phone and synced it to my mom's in dash GPS. He showed me how he did it then he pulled up YouTube on my phone and went to the rappers song. I listened to the song, and the production and lyrics were decent. It was nothing special about the rapper, he was just good not amazing. While listening to the song, I was thinking that we have rappers in St. Louis just as good as the dude Tae had me listening to.

It took us awhile to get to the liquor store. Stanley reassured me that we would be at the liquor store soon, but I started to have my doubts about his guidance. We finally pulled into a shopping plaza that had a variety of stores in it. One of the stores was a liquor store, and the focal point of the plaza was Kroger's Super Market. Stanley's brother darted straight for the Kroger's, while Stanley came with Tae and me into the liquor store.

I could tell that Tae had not been drinking that long. He had no idea what he wanted alcohol wise. He kept looking at the Remy Martin, Hennessey, and Jack Daniels. He did not know if he wanted to drink dark or white liquor, Gin or Tequila. I was on a budget. I knew I wanted dark liquor, so whatever dark liquor was cost efficient was going to be purchased. Stanley had the same mentality as I did. He purchased a couple of individual shot size containers of 3 various liquors. I myself purchased a fifth of

Crown Royal. I prefer Hennessey, but my budget would not let me be great that day.

Tae did not dispute my choice in alcohol. He did not put any money on the bottle, so he really had no choice but to be silent. I then surveyed the liquor store to find something for Crissy. I instinctively went to the wine section. I found some Moscato wine for $6.99. I had drunken it before, so I knew it tasted pretty good. After making the alcohol purchases, I left the liquor store and packed the product in the SUV. Stanley, Tae, and I then went into the Kroger's to finish my shopping. Stanley's brother was still missing, but I had a feeling he would find us before we left the Kroger's parking lot.

While we were walking through the Kroger's, Stanley told me that Memphis was a good city for black business. He said that the Kroger's was managed and run by mostly black people. I regret to say this, but this was not the case with many retail grocery store chains in St. Louis. It did not bother me too much. It was just food for thought that makes you think about the world you live in. Stanley then changed the whole dynamic of the conversation. He asked me if my aunt or uncles have ever mentioned him. I said, "No!" He then told me that he use to come to St. Louis all the time when he was younger. After that statement Stanley gave me his complete gangster resume. He told me he has sold dope and shot people. I took this information as no surprise. My uncles have their own personal street resumes, that I have heard stories about myself. They don't wear it as a badge of honor. Mainly because they are old now, so all the glory they had back in the day is over now. Stanley informing me of his past, and him hanging out with my uncles made perfect sense. There was no dispute in my mind that Stanley was truly about the life he spoke of.

Stanley then asked me another question that took me off guard. He asked me if my aunt still smoked weed. I mean I kind of knew she smoked weed, but I was not in any way prepared for this question. The aunt he spoke of was always the fun aunt, and I have actually found weed in her basement before. She just told me that it was my uncle's supply, and I did not ask any further questions. My reply to Stanley was that I have never smoked with her, but as far as I know she still smokes from time to time. Stanley just gave me a head nod. Shortly after that awkward conversation, we reached the Juice isle in the Kroger's.

I looked through the juice and soda section trying to figure out what I could get for Chaz and Bria. Stanley told me that I could give him the cash, and he would pay for the drinks on his food stamp card. I agreed to this then I gathered up $10 worth of juice and Gatorade. It was all at a good price, so I had 2 full arms of stuff to carry. When we got to checkout, Stanley bought the drinks with his card and I purchased an 89 cent candy bar to break the $20 bill Crissy gave me. I used the change I got, to cash Stanley out. I split the candy bar with Tae. I did not eat my half of the candy bar. I just stuffed it in cargo pants in the side pocket next to my thigh.

On our way out the Kroger's we saw Stanley's brother patiently waiting for us. He had purchased some ice, and a 24 pack of beer. My mom called me to see what was taking so long. I told her it took us longer to get to the liquor store than expected, but I was on my way back. When I got back to the barbecue I parked my mom's SUV in the exact spot I had pulled out of. I gave Crissy her change, put the kids drinks in the cooler, and I got me and Tae some cups with ice in it.

CHAPTER 4

I cracked open my bottle of Crown Royal once I got settled in. I made sure Crissy had a cup to drink her wine then I pulled me and Tae a drink out of my alcohol supply. My mom told me the food was ready. She had been helping get the barbecue under way since we got there. 90 minutes later everything was ready to go, and everyone could somewhat rest and eat. We all gathered in a circle, and prayed over the food before we started eating. I had enough respect to put my drink down, and take my hat off for the prayer. Once the prayer was done, everyone got into a line and started making their plates.

Earlier before we got to the barbecue, my granny said that she did not like my aunt Ping's cooking. This was a nonissue because Aunt Ping did not do any of the cooking for real. My cousins Yvette and Hazel did most the work. I got at the end of the food line, because I was not terribly hungry. I was not full from the Cracker Barrel brunch I had earlier that day, but I was not hungry either. I was just nourished. When I got the smell of the ribs though, my appetite came to and I was ready to eat.

Someone brought a table out the trailer and placed it where the initial half circle of chairs was at. My granny and Ping came out the trailer, and sat at the table. They had someone make their plates, and they started to eat their food. I sat with them. I swear once food came to the table, at least 23 flies came out of nowhere. They had not been there before, but once the smell of food was in the air the flies were not far behind. I fanned as many of them away as possible, but it was nearly hopeless. I did somehow get the flies to calm down long enough to enjoy my plate though.

I have a thing where I do not like to drink alcohol and eat food at the same time. Because of this I put my drinking on pause to eat my food. When me food was done, I was ready to drink. I had already taken some sips of my drink before I started eating, but I was in a different state of mind now. I was ready to go in. My mom came over to my table to be nosey about what I was drinking. She asked me what I was drinking, and I showed her the bottle of Crown Royal. She then asked me when I started drinking Crown Royal, like I was a child. I did not even answer her, I just kept drinking. While enjoying a social drink with Tae, I am 100 percent sure that once he drunk a few sips of the Crown Royal he was immediately buzzed. I did not take Tae for a light weight at first impression, but I guess looks are deceiving.

More people came once the food was in full effect. I drank my Crown Royal until I felt a warm feeling in my stomach. I did not want to be drunk at the family reunion, but I did not want to be completely sober either. I met a couple of other people including Hazel's son. When she introduced us, she told me about a whole memory I should have had that I did not recall. Hazel told me she came to St. Louis and me, her son, and 2 other people went to the mall together and took a picture. I had no memory of this. I really did not care for the story that much. I just listened to it, and shook her sons hand to be nice. Nothing else came from that conversation, just an awkward silence then I walked away.

I let the liquor wear off a little bit then Tae told me that his cousin had a basketball. I looked across the road and saw the outdoor basketball court. I knew it was time to hoop! We all crossed the street and jumped the fence to enter the court. I took Chaz with me also. I was concerned about Chaz jumping the fence, but he instinctively knew what to do when he saw the obstacle. He jumped over the fence like he was one of the older kids. Chaz was only 6, so he did not have a concept of the game of basketball. All he knew was that the game involved dribbling and shooting the ball in the basket.

Chaz watched me play mostly, but every once in while he would play defense on a kid with the ball. I brought some bottled water and Gatorade for us to drink while we played ball. This came in handy, because it was extremely hot that day. The half candy bar I had left in my side pocket of my pants melted almost soon as I left the Kroger's. I did not notice initially, but when I started stuffing bottles of water into my pockets, I realized the candy bar had almost liquefied. I had chocolate residue on the inside of my pocket and all over my headphones.

I got in a decent hooping session. The liquor was slowing me down, so I took frequent breaks. When I had enough I told Chaz we were going back to the barbecue. More people had come to the event. There was a DJ playing music, and it was clear that people were enjoying themselves. The barbecue was a success!

When I got back to the barbecue, I handed Chaz over to his mother. I had been wearing my tank top, so I went to the SUV to replace my sweaty shirt for a dry clean shirt. On my way back from the vehicle Crissy grabbed my arm and said, "It's some static happening, so we are about to leave soon!" I did not know what she meant. She did manage to find my mom, and to start rounding her kids up. When my mom got wind of the drama that was happening, she told my granny. My granny was not concerned at the situation. She just nodded her head at the information and continued to sit in her seat.

Once we got my granny out of the trailer, we assembled everyone to take a family reunion picture. We took about 3 pictures as a group before everyone dispersed. It started to get dark, so my immediate family packed into my mom's SUV. The darkness snuck up us. It went from day to night in a matter of 10 minutes.

When I was safely in the car, I asked my sister what was the static she spoke of. Crissy told me that one of the relatives had gotten into an argument with another relative. Being disrespected, one of the men went to their car to get his gun! Crissy then told me that the guy that went to get his gun told his alcoholic brother. Who also in turn went to get his gun! As we drove out of the parking space, past the barbecue, I told Crissy to point out the guy who had the gun. It was dark, but I managed to see who she was talking about. Of all the people it was Stanley and his brother.

It was a crowd of people leaving the barbecue, so we had to wait a considerable amount of time for the pathway to clear. While we were waiting, Crissy told me that the guy who Stanley was mad at had on a red hat. I was wearing a red hat that day, so she was concerned that Stanley and his brother would get drunk and start shooting it out. In the midst of their drunken behavior, they might confuse me with their intended target. This was farfetched, but it was possible! I chuckled at the situation, and my granny did the same. She said that she was too old to worry about all that nonsense.

I asked everyone in the SUV what the dispute was over. My mom spoke up and said that every adult that attended the barbecue was supposed to pay $25. Because Stanley brought his own food, he did not want to pay the fee. When my cousin Hazel found this out, she confronted him about the $25 fee. Her husband got involved then Stanley not paying became a big issue. Everything blew over, but we were on edge for at least 20 minutes.

When the pathway to the road cleared, we all said our final goodbyes, and headed back to the hotel. When I got back to the hotel, I text the girl I knew who lived in Memphis. Her name was Ardella. She was a cool person whom I had known for a number of years. She was petite in stature, and was on the natural hair wave that had been going on for a couple of years. She was into the frizzy fro, and frequently conditioned and greased her hair. She did not perm or relax her hair, nor did she wear weave. When she decided to go natural, her hair was not even that long. She stayed with it, and her hair blossomed into an amazing entity of its own. Her hair looked like it had its own personality, and she made it work with the different techniques she used to control it. We were just friends, but it was a definite connection that we had. I asked her, via text, what she was doing that night. She said she was going to the movies. She then text saying, that she could meet me on Beale Street once the movie was over.

Ardella asked me where my hotel was located. I told her Germantown. The reply I got back was a "WOW!" She lived 5 minutes from Beale Street, meaning she lived 30 minutes from my hotel. I told her, I could meet her at her apartment. She said OK, and told me that she would text me when she got out the movie.

This was a problem. I had actually driven the family from the barbecue to the hotel. My mom hackled me the whole drive. She asked me if I was drunk 6 times, tried to backseat drive about 3 times, and complained about how fast I was driving at least 8 times. She had gotten herself worked up over me driving, and the drive only lasted 15 minutes. I decided I would not drive with her in the car the rest of the trip.

Driving with my mom in the car reminded me when I was a teenager learning to drive. She was the worst teacher ever! My mom would weave in and out of traffic, speed, and switch lanes without using her blinker. This was fine for her, but once I did it she would raise all hell! Driving with her in the car was all around stressful. It was not until I got my own car and license, that I could tell my mom that the state of Missouri approves me to drive in the way I see fit. The drive back to the hotel was no different. It was my mom's vehicle, so she could complain about how it was being driven all she wanted.

I decided I was going to take my mom's SUV without her knowing, and tell her I got picked up. This plan was perfect, because I was not heading out to Beale Street until midnight. This meant that my mom and granny would be in bed sound asleep. What my mom did not know was not going to hurt her. I just had to execute.

About 30 minutes before I left, I put on my outfit for the night. I did not know what I was about to get into, so I dressed for any occasion. I had on a nice pair of jeans, a button up shirt, and loafers with no socks. I was prepared to party anywhere, in whatever fashion. I got Ardella's address via text, and grabbed my mom's keys. While I sat in the driver seat of my mom's SUV, plugging the address into the GPS, I thought to myself that I was going to be in serious trouble if I got caught. I then finished plugging the coordinates into the GPS, and headed out.

It took me 25 minutes to get to the general area Ardella lived in. I could not find her apartment complex, so I called her. We agreed that we would meet at a nearby

Churches Chicken parking lot. Ardella was being driven by the guy she went to the movies with. I did not recognize the car when it pulled up next to me on the parking lot. I was concerned for a little bit, but once Ardella poked her head out the window all the anxiety I built up was diminished. I followed the car to Beale Street, and we found a parking lot where both of us could park fairly close to each other.

When I parked the SUV, sitting in the position I was in, I could not see where Ardella and her friend parked. I decided to call Ardella, but I accidentally called my mom instead. When I realized my mistake, I immediately ended the call. It was too little too late, because my mom called me right back. The jig was up! I thought I was in major trouble. My mom asked me where I was at. I told her I was on Beale Street. She said, "OK" then instructed me to be careful. She did not know I took her car, and I planned to keep it like that!

After the conversation with my mom was over, Ardella and her friend walked up on the SUV. She introduced me to him, and said his name was Mike. He was a cool dude. He was kind of stocky with a thick beard, but he was dressed nice so I assumed he was a respectable guy. I did not get the vibe that Ardella and Mike was on a true date, but they were definitely having a date like experience. I did not want to be the third wheel, but both of them made me feel comfortable. I asked Mike how he knew Ardella. He told me that he was in a fraternity. Some members of his fraternity met with some members of Ardella's sorority on Beale Street after a greek picnic. After meeting at the rendezvous, they were friends ever since.

We walked to Beale Street. There was a police barricade at the entrance to the street. There also was a line formed outside the barricade, were police officers were checking everyone who entered into Beale Street. We hopped in line, and waited until it was our turn to be checked. I looked at what the people of Memphis were wearing. I immediately noticed I was overdressed. I mean Ardella, Mike, and I looked nice, but a dress code was nonexistent. I could have worn my basketball shorts and been just fine.

Once I got to the entrance of the police barricade, I was patted down then allowed entry into Beale Street. The street was popping! It was summertime, and people were out enjoying themselves. It was a host of attractive and non-attractive females that I was able to witness. The mixture of people was amazing. I saw a plethora of black people, but every single nationality was represented in some type of way.

While walking down the street, I noticed a lot of bars had the outdoor/indoor bar setup. You could purchase drinks from an establishment without ever having to enter into the building. Since the police carded people at the entrance to Beale Street, there was no problem in serving anyone who came to purchase liquor on the out-door bar. Immediately upon getting onto the street, we went to one of the outdoor bars. Mike bought a round of drinks for everyone. I did not turn it down. I just told him I would get the next round.

We walked up and down the street inhaling the Memphis environment. I got to catch up with Ardella. I asked her about her life in Memphis, and how everything was going. She told me that she was working 2 jobs, doing freelance work as a personal trainer, and taking online classes for graduate school. She did not have a boyfriend, but she had gone on multiple dates since being transplanted in the city. She then scuffled through her blazer and handed me her business card for her personal training business. She told me to take it back to St. Louis and show it to all of her former coworkers.

After hearing about Ardella's fast pace life I purchased another round of drinks. Mike offered to pay for the round, but I told him I had it taken care of. Ardella told me that all the men she recently met were southern gentlemen. She described how she could not pay for any meals or drinks. Also the men would get the door for her, and pull out her chair before she sat down. I looked at her and said, "WOW!" I was from the Midwest. I was taught chivalry, but it had a limitation. I had no problem paying for a woman's meal on a date, but I'm not going to do everything for her. To be honest, most women I have encountered would complain about a guy doing too much, and see that as a sign of weakness. I have never truly dealt with a southern woman, so my way of thinking was purely regional.

Ardella saw the look in my eyes, and she knew what I was thinking. She was familiar with the mentality of women I had grown accustomed to. She explained to me how in St. Louis she was raised to do for herself. Her reasoning was if a man does something for you then he will want something in return. Ardella said she had this mentality when she moved to Memphis. After meeting multiple men who had the southern gentlemen way of living, she realized she was being exposed to a new culture. I was still in culture shock, but I was only visiting. I would be fine once I got back to St. Louis, and started texting the same women I usually text.

After I finished my second drink, Mike bought me another one. He was trying to put me on edge. I had gotten relaxed, and started to adjust to my surroundings quite rapidly. Mike introduced me to one of his friends he grew up with. I did not remember the guy's name, but I do remember how he looked. He was about 6'1, and his lining could be compared to that of Dwayne "The Rock" Johnson. Other than that, he was a young black man like Mike and I.

Upon me talking to Mike's friend, I noticed he had a little bit of black activist in him. He and Mike grew up in a small town in Tennessee an hour away from Memphis. Both of them went to college, got degrees, and were currently in the process of bettering themselves. During the course of our conversation, I asked Mike's friend what he thought about student loans. Earlier that night Mike told me he got his student loans expunged. He instructed me to talk to his friend to get more information on the subject. Mike's friend told me that during the process of filling out the FAFSA, you have to electronically sign a document. Apparently that electronic signature is not a valid signature. Knowing this loophole, he made an appeal with the small claims court. His appeal was denied, so he sent another one. Once his case was heard, he asked the judge if the crediting company had a legal document stating that he owed the specified amount of money. The judge reviewed the document, and told the representative of the crediting agency he had a week to come up with legal documentation. After a week the representative of the company did not show. The judge had no choice but to expunge the loan.

The information I had just heard was hard for me to believe. I expressed doubt in my body language, so Mike's friend told me to reference a book. The name of the book was Commercial and Debt or Credit Law. He told me that if I read the language in the book carefully, I would see what he was talking about. I recorded all the information mentally then resumed drinking my drink.

At some point in the night Ardella said she had to use the restroom. So Ardella, Mike, Mike's friend, and I walked over to the area the public restroom was in. The restroom area sat back off the main street, and was like a side court that had its own space. It sat between 2 buildings, and there was a sculpture in the middle of the court. To the left of the sculpture was a Barbeque stand along with a men and women restroom.

Ardella went into the women restroom, and I waited by the sculpture until she was done. While I was waiting for Ardella I lost track of Mike. I knew he had not gone far, but I could not see him. All of sudden a crowd of people rushed into the court! Most of the women ran into the women's restroom, and some of the guys ran into the men's restroom. I stepped out the way of the mob. I assumed someone had gotten shot, but I did not hear a gunshot! After 10 minutes of chaos Ardella found me standing by the sculpture. She asked me what happed. From her vantage point, she just saw a bunch of people rush into the restroom while she was inside of it. I told her I was not sure, but I did not hear a gunshot. Ardella shrugged it off, and we found Mike and his friend by the Barbeque stand.

Mike's friend told me the barbeque stand I was standing next to was the best barbeque in Memphis. My initial observation of the food stand was that it was nothing but Africans cooking the food. I was not sure if I wanted to eat there, but after short consideration I decided to roll the dice and give it a try. I stood in line, with Ardella, waiting to be serviced.

Before we got to the front counter I asked Ardella what she was eating. Ardella usually eats clean, and does not eat greasy fattening food. This night she had been drinking, so she was fine with taking a break from her usual eating habits. She did keep her strict policy of not eating pork. This cut her options of food drastically! She was restricted to about 5 items on the menu. I felt bad for her, but it was her choice. I personally did not plan on giving up pork until I was 30 years of age. Ardella got some chicken, and I got a pulled pork sandwich.

My pulled pork sandwich was cold when I got it. I was feeling the effects of the alcohol, so I was too buzzed to complain about my food. I put some cold slaw and barbeque sauce on my sandwich. I had never eaten a sandwich with this combination of food, and it was amazing! Even though the meat was cold, the sandwich was awesome.

I ate my sandwich then I was ready to go. I was full of food and liquor, and my day had been quite eventful. I walked back to the SUV with Mike and Ardella. Beale Street was starting to empty out, and there was a constant stream of people walking to their vehicles. Ardella and Mike saw some people they knew, and asked them about the commotion that happened earlier that night. One of guys said someone got shot outside the police barricade. It made sense to me, but I still did not hear a gunshot.

When I got back to my vehicle I hugged Ardella and shook Mike's hand. Ardella told me to text her when I got back to the hotel. I then hopped in the SUV and drove off. I followed the GPS all the way back to the hotel. It was a 30 minute drive, and I was semi-drunk. All I could think about was what if I got pulled over, or what if I crash the truck. My level of anxiety was at an all time high. I kept it together long enough to make it to my destination. I had both hands on the wheel, and I watched the road thoroughly. Once I pulled into the hotel, I checked to see if I could get the same parking spot I had before I left. Luckily it was still there! Outside the amount of gas I used, there was no evidence I had taken the SUV.

When I got back in my room my granny was up. Old people are always awake at weird times of the night. She asked me what I was doing. I laughed and told her I just got back in from going out. She looked at me then climbed back into her bed. I changed clothes, and prepared my place on the couch. I did not let the bed out, because it was more comfortable to sleep on the couch cushions. I set the alarm on my phone and quickly went to sleep.

CHAPTER 5

The next day my phone woke me up in enough time to catch the continental breakfast. I just got a croissant and some frosted flakes because I did not trust the eggs or the sausage. My granny wanted breakfast also, so she came with me. She got some sausage, toast, and coffee. I helped her get everything she needed then helped her back to the hotel room.

Helping my granny was always an interesting experience. I could never really gage how much she could really do. If I left it up to her, she would try to do everything herself. If I allowed for this to happen, and something goofy happened like a fall, I would be blamed for the rest of time for her mishap or injury. This particular time, my granny kept misplacing her cane. She scooped her eggs up and poured her coffee just fine. She was moving around the buffet area like she was back in the kitchen at my mom's house. We actually got in an out pretty smooth. We almost got out the buffet area, when I realized my granny walked to the continental breakfast with a cane. I let my granny keep walking, and I found her cane lying on the floor by the coffee area. I snatched it up, and caught up with her. There was going no blame on my hands for anything!

Checkout was at noon, so we had a bit of time to eat our breakfast and relax. I ate my cereal and packed my bags. I made sure I had all my shoes, my phone charger, and my watch. Once everything was checked off, I was good to go. I got the luggage cart, and began loading everyone's luggage onto it. When I loaded my granny's oxygen tank I was very careful. The day before, I managed to jab myself in the forehead with the thin metal point that covered the top of the tank. I did not let this happen again! I had a whole flesh wound that was still healing.

Once everything was loaded, I pushed the cart to Crissy's room. She loaded her and the kid's luggage. After everyone's possessions were accounted for, I pushed the cart out to the hotel lobby. I waited for my mom and sister to checkout then went outside and drove the SUV to the entrance of the hotel. We packed the vehicle with the luggage and were ready to go.

I do not know why the departure from the hotel was not smooth after that point. I just remember the kids, my granny, and I were waiting in the SUV for at least 15 minutes. Bria had an orange in her hand, and she was trying to decide if she wanted to eat it or not. I was in the driver seat, so I pulled the SUV into a parking spot near the door. The reason for the wait still eludes me. All I know is when my mom and Crissy got to the car, we packed in and drove away.

First we stopped at Aunt Ping's house. It was the same place the barbecue was held, so the coordinates were already set in the GPS. When we arrived, Stanley and his immediate family were there also. My granny and mom went inside the trailer to say by to Ping. I stayed outside and spoke with Stanley and couple of other people who were there. There was only 1 dog this time. The other dog was nowhere to be seen. The one dog that was out, was limping. Stanley said that dog and the other dog got into a fight, and the dog I was looking at had gotten bit on the leg. He pointed out how it was favoring one of its back legs, and I felt sorry for the little thing.

Stanley told me he did not have a hotel, and he stayed at Ping's house through the course of the weekend. He then asked me what I did the previous night. I informed him I had gone to Beale Street. He asked me how I got there, and I lied and told him I got picked up. He seemed slightly disappointed. He told me that after the people left the barbecue it was boring. He also mentioned that he had people mad at him, because of the confrontation with Hazel's husband.

During the course of the conversation one of the relatives asked me about my uncles. He was very familiar with each and every one of them. I filled him in as best as I could. Fortunately for me, before any question was asked that I could not answer my mom and granny came out the trailer. They said it was time to go and wished everyone farewell. My granny had a couple of collectables in her hand. It was pots to grow plants in. In my grandmothers old age she liked to cook and grow plants. I did not know why she needed more pots, but there was no point in asking her either. I carefully packed the clay pots on top of the luggage and kept it moving.

We packed into the SUV once again and headed to our final destination in Memphis. It was the home of the king! GRACELAND!!!!!!!!! We had been to Graceland the other day, so getting back was nearly not as big an obstacle. We did go the wrong way on the highway for 2 exits, but we quickly corrected our path.

When we pulled up to Graceland it was $10 to park. I contributed to the parking fee, and we parked in the handicap section. It was late in the day, and my granny was really dragging. She was feeling the effects of poor dieting during the trip. Her kidneys did not work, so if she ate and drank too much of the wrong things fluid would build up in her body. It would put pressure on her heart and lungs, causing her to feel sluggish and out of breath. She hooked up her portable oxygen in preparation for the rest of the day. The oxygen was there to give her relief until she was able to make her next dialysis appointment.

My mom suggested we use the scooter. We had not used the scooter the entire trip. It was a waste of room until this point. It was a look of relief on my mom's face when she saw me pull the scooter out the back of the SUV. It took me a couple of minutes to set it up. While I was assembling the scooter, my mom was laying down some ground rules for my granny. She told her to be courteous of people, and not to run over everybody and everything. My granny was notorious for having no regard for anyone when she got in her scooter. Her 2 favorite places were the grocery store and casino. She would drive through the aisles leaving a trail of destruction. In the casino there are chairs arranged in a line facing each slot machine. My granny would use her scooter to ram the space between 2 chairs until there was room for her to use the slot the machine. In the grocery store, she would cruise down the middle of the isle at full speed making everyone in her path move out the way. Knowing this information my mom did not want any problems out of my granny when she finally got to ride her scooter.

When we got to the entrance of the main lobby, we noticed that the tour of Elvis mansion cost an additional fee. It was like $33 for an adult and $15 for a child between 7 and 12. My granny looked at the prices displayed on the standing billboard, and turned her nose up. She said we can pay to see whatever we wanted, but she was not having any parts of it. My mom said that Crissy, the kids, and I could go, and she and my granny would wait for us to get done.

There was a basic tour of the mansion, but for $5 extra we could do the platinum tour. This tour included Elvis' planes and 2 extra museums. Crissy and I decided to pay the extra $5. They already were getting almost 40 bucks out of us, what was 5 more dollars. When I got to the window the cashier told me it was a discount for AAA Car Service members. I had an old AAA card my mom had given me 2 years ago. It had been expired for nearly a year. The cashier was cool. She did not ask too many questions, and gave me the discount. Crissy on the other hand had a cashier that was not trying to give her a break at all. Our cashiers were not that the faraway from each other, so when she found out about the AAA discount she asked me for my card. Her cashier told her the card was expired and she would not accept it. Also seeing how tall Bria was, she asked her how old she was when Crissy was not paying attention. All of this coupled with the cashier giving Crissy a suspicious look when she told her Chaz was 6 years old. Ultimately Crissy paid full price for her and Bria, and Chaz got in for free. Bria's ticket was around $20 and Crissy's was $38. Crissy was disappointed she had to pay so much to view the Elvis estate. She made plans to eat some Memphis barbecue from an establishment on Beale Street. After she was done paying for the tour, she cut her loses and canceled the plans for barbecue.

Comparing Crissy and I, we were from 2 different generations. She was 18 years older than me. My respect for Elvis was that of a legend. I paid homage to what he did for the music industry. Also I was interested in learning how Elvis was able to brand and market himself in the 50's. Crissy being older listened to Elvis' albums and watched all the movies he was in. She actually remembered him being alive! He was fat and out of shape at that point in her life, but he was alive none the less.

As part of the platinum tour we would do the mansion tour first then everything else would follow later. It was a 20 minute wait to catch the bus that was taking us to the mansion. While we waited, I looked at the diagram of the mansion in the pamphlet I grabbed from the main lobby. There was also an opportunity to take a picture before we boarded the bus to the mansion. Crissy, the kids, and I huddled together and took a group picture. Shortly after that, it was our time to board the bus. Before our bus came, we received headphones attached to a recorder. The recorder had the narration for the tour recorded on it. We also had the option to pause the narration when or wherever we needed to.

The bus dropped us off outside the mansion. We had to wait a couple of minutes before we could enter. One of the guides told us what buttons to press on the recorder, so that we could begin the tour on the correct part of the recorder. After the guide checked to see if everyone had their recorders set, we entered into the mansion.

Elvis moved into that mansion in the 50's. He was definitely living the life! His house looked better than people's houses they have now. The tour included all the rooms of the house, except Elvis' bedroom. The recorder said Elvis kept the upstairs to his home private while he was alive, so out of respect the room remains private till this very day.

The tour went into detail when explaining the purpose and design of each room. After we saw all the rooms on the main level we went to the basement. The basement had a bar style setting, with an assortment of retro couches facing 3 old school television sets. The recorder said the reason Elvis had 3 TVs next to each other, was because back in the day there were only 3 TV stations. Elvis wanted to look at all the channels simultaneously. This was hilarious to me. Even back in the 50's and 60's stunting was something that was prevalent in society.

We left the main house and headed to the backyard. The yard was amazing! It was large and spacious. Not to mention that Elvis had a decked out pool. The pool had marble tile lined on the edges, and there were benches arranged around it. It looked like a cool spot to hang out. The recorder mentioned that Elvis had such a large yard, because he and his friends liked to ride motorized go carts around his property. There was a painting dedicated to this fun, and it made it easy to visualize the fun Elvis potentially had.

In the backyard area was a guest house. Part of the guest house was used as an office for Elvis' manager. At first glance the office looked messy. This was surreal seeing that managers for musicians have a lot to deal with. They do so much backline work, and the artist gets all the fame. This was no different back then, and it is no different now. Past the office were stairs that went down into a large room. The room was so large that the ceiling went up 2 stories instead of 1. You could look down into the entire room from the top of the stairs. From my view I could see couches and tables arranged in a social setting. The recorder said Elvis used the room to entertain guest at his estate. Also it served as a waiting area for the racket ball court he had in the next room.

The racket ball room was the only room in the whole mansion estate which was greatly altered. It was no longer a racket ball court, but a tribute to Elvis's life. There were TVs playing interviews Elvis did while he was alive. Also there were a couple of album covers and rewards Elvis received. My favorite part of the room was the life size replica of Elvis in the middle of the display. I felt obligated to take a picture with the replica. It just seemed right. The mansion tour was amazing so far. For $33 I really did not have a doubt if the money was worth it. I would have liked to pay less, but the experience was well received.

Lastly before we left the mansion grounds we got to see Elvis burial site. He was buried in the backyard of his mansion estate next to his mom and dad. Know thinking about it, being buried in your backyard is kind of weird. Obviously Elvis was not the typical person, but the memorial dedicated to him and his parents was dope. They kept fresh flowers around his grave, and the head-stones were crisp and untarnished. I tried to take a good picture of it with my phone, but it was hard because of the multitude of people surrounding the grave site.

The tour was over and we left the backyard area to return to the front of the mansion. We had some time to take pictures in front of the mansion before the bus came. Crissy made sure I got a picture of her and the kids. I was gone take one of myself in front of the mansion, but I knew I would not like the picture. I elected to take the pictures Crissy wanted then we could go back to the entrance to Graceland.

When we got back to the main Graceland area our platinum tour allowed us to see 2 more museums, and the plane. We first went to the car museum. Chaz had a problem staying with the group. He kept running off, and I was concerned! I looked at Crissy, and she acted like it was normal. I told Chaz to stay with the group twice then I was done with it. I was trying to see what Elvis was driving.

I am not sure the make and model of all the cars Elvis had in his possession, but it is clear to say Elvis had cars on top of cars. Each vehicle was top of the line, for vehicles at that time. I was educating myself on the multitude of vintage cars Elvis had, when a security guard saw Chaz touching the display area beyond the velvet ropes. She was a tall woman, and she said there were sensors all around the exhibits. Crissy went over to Chaz while he was getting yelled at, and she scolded him. She told him to stay with her, and not run off anymore.

After leaving the car museum we went to the other museum area. This exhibit focused on Elvis performance wear and movies he stared in. Apparently Elvis was very profound in the way he dressed. The exhibit highlighted each aspect of the costumes Elvis preformed in. Along with the multiple of manikins wearing Elvis's outfits, there was a hall that had all of Elvis platinum and gold albums. This hallway was immensely long! Elvis had so many hits. It felt like it took me 10 minutes to walk down this hallway. The musical achievements were almost endless. Along with the platinum albums and the theatrical performances Elvis was involved in, all this exhibit did was confirm Elvis Presley was that dude.

We lastly visited the Elvis plane and jet display. My mom sent a text asking how much longer we were going to be. I replied by saying that after we saw the plane exhibit we could leave. We walked to the plane, and it was every bit interesting as the mansion. Elvis had a dining table with a retro fridge sitting on the edge of it. The video next to the fridge said Elvis liked Gatorade and soda. It even said that alcohol was not all that favorable to him. I found this ironic, seeing Elvis died of a drug overdose. I guess him not being fond of alcohol left room for other drugs to be used in its absence.

We left the dining room area, and entered the next section of the plane. I noticed couches and seats arranged like that of a living room. It was weird seeing this on a plane. All the planes I have ridden on were commercial flights. I could not imagine having my own plane, let alone being able to design and decorate it to my liking. Making a plane look like a home would be insane to me! None the less I absorbed the ambiance of Elvis' wealth.

I continued on the tour, and saw the bedroom Elvis had at the tail end of the plane. All the furniture was wrapped in plastic, so I thought I could touch it. I was just about to sit in a cushioned seat then I read a sign that said "NO TOUCHING!" In the midst of me reading the sign, my hand was resting on the chair. I quickly removed it, and walked to the end of the plane. Before I exited, I saw a barber's station. It was actually inside a restroom. I could not walk into the station, but I did see a mirror faucet, and counter.

The jet was the last thing we had to see before the Graceland experience was over. After seeing the luxurious plane, I knew the jet had to be on the same level or even better. When I got to the jet, I could not walk through the inside of the aircraft. There was a glass wall separating the tourist from the passenger part of the jet. The cockpit was also segregated in a similar fashion. There was just a small section of the jet you could walk into and do a complete 360 turn. I looked through both glass walls for a total of 2 minutes. This was the most disappointing part of the whole tour. It was just not up to par with the other attractions. After I got my fill, I found all my family members and joined them outside the entrance to Graceland.

Overall my Graceland experience was a 7.8 out of 10. This was because for the price I paid, I did not get to spend as much time as I wanted to spend in the museum areas. My mom and grandma rushed me! My granny was not feeling good, so the sooner we got home the better. It could have been way worse though.

I helped load my granny's scooter back into the SUV. Shortly after loading up, we headed straight for St. Louis. My mom was driving, so it was pedal to the metal the whole way home. As we drove past downtown Memphis, it was like a feeling of accomplishment as we left the city. The trip was drawing to an end, and everyone had made it including my granny!

We stopped in Arkansas to redeem the scratch off tickets my granny bought earlier that weekend. Off course my granny bought more tickets. Everyone else used the pit stop to get something to eat. It was a McDonalds located next to the gas station. I eat McDonalds……so I ordered me some food, and I watched while Crissy ordered Bria and Chaz something to eat. I was 25 years of age, and never was fond of McDonald's chicken nuggets.

I tried them once when I was little, and told my dad I wanted a Quarter Pounder with cheese. He did not try to persuade me otherwise, he just said OK and that was the end of the McDonalds chicken nuggets. Chaz and Bria were inhaling them. Chaz does not eat that much, so he ate a few of them. Bria, on the other hand, ate all the nuggets she was offered.

While we were sitting down and eating, my mom found us inside the McDonalds. She asked us how much longer we had to go. We just looked at each other, and started wrapping up our meal. We walked to the SUV collectively as a family. My granny was sitting on a bench outside the McDonalds. In her hand was a stack of lottery tickets. She had sat outside and scratched off all those lottery tickets, while we were eating inside the McDonalds. I asked my granny if she won. She looked at me and said, "Shoot! They all losers!" It did not surprise me, but she insisted she was done playing scratch offs for the day.

We packed into the SUV for the last time, and headed towards St. Louis. When we got to St. Louis, near my mom's house, my granny was asleep. My mom drove briskly past the liquor store, because she did not want to stop anymore before she got home. She told me she would take my granny to turn in the rest of her tickets later in the week.

After we pulled up to the house Brandi was patiently waiting on us. She helped my granny into the house. She also made a comment on how swollen my granny's legs were. The fluid buildup in her body was staring to show through on her physical appearance. It was good she was going to dialysis the next day. Brandi just looked at her and said, "Looks like yal barely made it." She was right! With everything that happened, we were blessed to be home safely.

I gathered my belongings and packed it into my car. Brandi washed my car, so it was shinny and crisp when we were reunited. I thanked her for all her hard work, and headed back to my apartment. I did not think too much about the trip as a whole after that. I just was trying to get home and get some rest for the next day at work. I finally made it to my bed and fell into my slumbers. My 3 day weekend was over, and I survived!

CPSIA information can be obtained
at www.ICGtesting.com
Printed in the USA
FFOW04n2017250615
14642FF

9 781457 537387